⇒ *Life's Little Deconstruction Book* ⇐

ALSO BY ANDREW BOYD

The Activist Cookbook

LIFE'S LITTLE DECONSTRUCTION BOOK

Self-help for the post-hip

ANDREW BOYD

W. W. Norton & Company
New York • London

Copyright © 1999 by Andrew Boyd

For information about permission to reproduce selections from this book, write to Permissions,
W. W. Norton & Company, Inc., 500 Fifth Avenue, New York, NY 10110.

The text of this book is composed in Weiss. Composition by Stephen Kaldon.
Book design by Charlotte Staub. Manufacturing by The Courier Companies, Inc.

Library of Congress Cataloging-in-Publication Data

Boyd, Andrew, 1962–
Life's little deconstruction book : self-help for the post-hip /
Andrew Boyd.
p.   cm.
Includes bibliographical references (p.).
ISBN 0-393-31870-2 (pbk.)
1. Conduct of Life—Humor.   2. Deconstruction—Humor.
3. Postmodernism—Humor.   I. Title.
N6231.C6142B69   1998
818'.5402—dc21   98-34020
                                                CIP

W. W. Norton & Company, Inc., 500 Fifth Avenue, New York, N.Y. 10110
http://www.wwnorton.com

W. W. Norton & Company Ltd., 10 Coptic Street, London WC1A 1PU

1 2 3 4 5 6 7 8 9 0

Acknowledgments

To Michael Barrish for his relentless editing and uncommon friendship.
To Janice Fine for her shakabookoo in the sushi bar.
To Liz Canner for her post-modern call to arms.
To Ken Jordan for his support and bulls-eye counsel.
To Kosta Demos for his polymath generosity.
To Alane Mason for her patience, shared vision, and democratic sensibilities.
And to mom and dad for my initial encoding and then some.
To each of you, I commemorate the following
imperatives, respectively:
279, 135, 295, 363, 144, 337, 10, 170.

1.

Talk about anything in the context
of anything else.

2.

Implicate yourself in every interpretation.

3.

Dip into nihilism.

4.

Sample.

5.

Need what recently didn't exist.

6.

Expose depth as another surface.

7.
Pose.

8.
Control the remote.

9.
Read the text as you desire.

10.

Learn to play a financial instrument.

11.

Bathe in an image of the natural.

12.

Play each role in good faith.

13.

Publicize your privates.

14.
Pretend to be real.

15.
Fashion reason.

16.
Reason about fashion.

17.
Participate without belonging.

18.

Disenchant.

19.

Be as different from the Joneses as you can afford.

20.

Dissolve truth into a patchwork of
language games.

21.
Indicate absence.

22.
Beg the question.

23.
Debt-finance immediate gratification.

24.

Resist—only to find yourself disarmed
and reabsorbed.

25.

Inflate.

26.

Disdain theorists.

27.
Don't seek the whole.

28.
Confuse art and advertising.

29.
Replace your models *of* reality with
models *as* reality.

30.
Sport amused, matter-of-fact cynicism.

31.
Withdraw into shell-shocked blasé.

32.
Helplessly and forever, contain the Other.

33.

Be as if.

34.
Reformat.

35.
Speak to be spoken—language composes you.

36.
Maneuver between pastiche and mishmash.

37.

Don't despair at the absurd, go with it.

38.

Regard conversation with the prestige once
reserved for inquiry.

39.

Perform your gender.

40.
Disregard the intentions of dead authors.

41.
Supplant the original.

42.
Scrutinize power.

43.
Suspend belief.

44.
Write more about less.

45.
Complicate race.

46.
Shop as though money were a
consensual hallucination.

47.

Stake all on the charisma of the storytellers.

48.

Reduce meaning to a hodgepodge of signifiers.

49.

Enjoy plural sexualities.

50.

Lay claim to one fragment.

51.
Move laterally.

52.
Read provisionally.

53.
Repurpose symbols of power.

54.

Log on in search of community.

55.

Lip-synch.

56.

Beware: history speaks of goals never intended.

57.

Voice subjugated discourses.

58.
Entertain alienation.

59.
Be a willy-nilly citizen of the world.

60.
Share nothing with strangers but an obsession
with celebrities.

61.

Refine your signal-to-noise ratio.

62.

Think where you cannot say you are.

63.

Without history, without heroes, rebel against the
blindness of information.

64.

Imitate Disneyworld.

65.
Learn from Las Vegas.

66.
Do something, anything, to attract
highly mobile capital.

67.
Rework what others have exhausted.

68.
Go digital.

69.
Go postal.

70.
Write texts that undermine their own authority.

71.
Play the game.

72.

Dress as tourists imagine.

73.

Turn over your beliefs as fast as your assets.

74.

Treat rationality as just another tradition.

75.

Profit from tastes you recently helped establish.

76.
Disorder taxonomies.

77.
Collapse hierarchy.

78.
Privatize truth.

79.
Question what belongs on the inside.

80.
Pursue multiple narratives that neither explain
nor unify.

81.
Cultivate decade-by-decade nostalgia.

82.

Show your work.

83.
Pose reality as an interesting hypothesis.

84.
Help yourself.

85.
Think again.

86.
Schmooze.

87.
Take the kids to see a replica of what never was.

88.
Be profoundly superficial.

89.
Cross borders.

90.
Negotiate identity.

91.

Look at, not into.

92.

Legitimate your own.

93.

Wallow in an orgy of information.

94.

Refer to what refers.

95.

Open up an abyss of infinite analytical regress.

96.
Rent a cop.

97.
Pass judgment without criteria.

98.
Be *ad hoc*.

99.
Name the ruling metaphor.

100.
Tweak your consciousness.

101.
Devalue.

102.
Remember: there are no facts, only
interpretations.

103.
Edit the images you inhabit.

104.
Reinscribe what you can't surpass.

105.
Dismiss utopia.

106.

Live in a building that quotes other buildings.

107.
Speculate.

108.
Don't answer to a single standard.

109.
Trace meaning further and further back.

110.
Let stories do their thing.

111.
Float globally, frame locally.

112.
Treat your body as a surface for transgression.

113.
Proliferate secondhand truths.

114.
Come out.

115.
Confer philosophical status on
linguistic gimmicks.

116.
Scan.

117.
Milk celebrity.

118.

Lose the center.

119.
Keep open your options for prejudice.

120.
Await catastrophe.

121.
Celebrate intensity.

122.
Blur the boundary between high and low.

123.
Watch your critical gaze slide into
ironic self-consciousness.

124.
Experiment in public.

125.
Exhibit the mark of the Other.

126.

Reconsider the artist—no longer a tormented heroic soul, but a well-heeled power broker.

127.

Speak not of reason, only reasons.

128.

Shuffle fragments.

129.
Hack.

130.
Package community.

131.
Design your own rituals.

132.

To change what things mean, redescribe them.

133.

Don't struggle, just enjoy the seduction.

134.

Beware: every decoding is another encoding.

135.

Displace the canon with attitude.

136.
Misread.

137.
Purchase genuine imitations.

138.
Disperse yourself in a cloud of narrative elements.

139.
Continue the tradition of breaking with tradition.

140.
Break with the tradition of breaking
with tradition.

141.
Follow the market.

142.
With clipped slogans and depthless images,
diminish the world.

143.
Gate your community.

144.
Vote anyway.

145.
Trouble your foundations.

146.
Network.

147.

Name what names you.

148.
Find purpose without direction.

149.
Affirm that some truth is still possible,
though a final truth is not.

150.
Fight for attention.

151.

Redeploy the images that oppose you.

152.

Study everything that can be used to tell a lie.

153.

Displace the universal human subject.

154.

Pervert.

155.

Splinter consensus.

156.

Reject ideal meanings—even the purest ideas
betray the impurities of language.

157.
Market anti-establishment postures.

158.
Care less who has power than how its effects
have made you.

159.
Mix codes.

160.
Read deeply into pop.

161.
Don't probe, just indulge your fascinations.

162.
Take pleasure.

163.

Slip into modernism.

164.
Reset your biological clock.

165.
Usurp reality.

166.
Implode metaphysics.

167.
Decipher signs by the trace of all in each.

168.

Mass produce difference.

169.
Borrow at will.

170.
Advance science through chaos, error, deviation.

171.
Speak in a different voice.

172.

Treat history as a continuum of
portable accessories.

173.

Treat history as an endless reserve of
equal events.

174.

Treat history as a resource bank of images for
casual reuse.

175.
Mock your own urgency.

176.
Temp.

177.
Long for a place to stash your electronic money.

178.
Approach the same horizon as the machine.

179.
Await the return of the repressed.

180.
Numb your capacity for outrage.

181.
Hemorrhage paradigms.

182.
Complicate the self-evident.

183.
Iterate.

184.
Design products with instant heritage.

185.

Unseat nature.

186.
Cut and paste.

187.
Bank.

188.
Integrate globally, disintegrate locally.

189.
Negotiate temporary contracts with both your
employer and your spouse.

190.
Tell lots of small stories.

191.

Use the word *deconstruction* without being quite sure whether it is a rigorous strategy for reversing the classic hierarchies of Western philosophy or a trendy academic parlor trick.

192.

Mess around.

193.

Outsource.

194.

Inscribe.

195.
Visit the public square on your private screen.

196.
Expand your possibilities and your sense of
inadequacy.

197.
Accessorize your rebellion.

198.
Leave the *avant garde* behind.

199.
Do it yourself.

200.
Make fine distinctions about things that
don't matter.

201.
Collect world views.

202.
Watch all that is solid melt into air.

203.
Favor aesthetics over ethics, rhetoric over reason.

204.
Bomb smart.

205.

Manufacture nostalgia.

206.
Define your self in the mirror of the excluded,
silenced Other.

207.
Confuse the original and the copy.

208.
Write texts your readers can rewrite.

209.
Hedge.

210.
Never arrive.

211.
In wartime, watch video games on
the nightly news.

212.
Expose the codes by which corporate meanings
become our own.

213.

Be wherever, whenever.

214.

Occasionally pause the endless cycle of
interpretation.

215.

Make room for absence.

216.
Label your tribe.

217.
Abandon the future to fantasies of social collapse.

218.
Buy a home built as much for fiction as function.

219.
Saturate.

220.
Be entertained by information, informed by
entertainment.

221.

In the attempt to demystify, further obscure.

222.
Have a taste for all the world's cuisines.

223.
Imagine you're a nomadic, desiring machine,
without limits.

224.
Forsake Marx, embrace Nietzsche.

225.

Defer identity.

226.

Play with texts while an oppressive social system goes about its business.

227.

Choose religion cafeteria-style.

228.

Live without a big picture.

229.

Transgress.

230.
Politicize your aesthetics,
aestheticize your politics.

231.
Watch your fiercest critique become the
latest rage.

232.
Switch channels.

233.
Rehash.

234.
Rehash.

235.
Lower the common denominator.

236.
Open your body to technology.

237.

Be wary of stories that presume to judge other
stories.

238.

Guarantee nothing.

239.

Restructure your feelings.

240.

Take irony for granted.

241.
Preserve your heritage through
aggressive marketing.

242.
Morph.

243.
Don't believe the hype.

244.
Make a spectacle of yourself.

245.
Instead of absolute truth,
seek infinite dissemination.

246.
Empower difference.

247.
Saw the branch on which you sit.

248.
Invest globally, deindustrialize locally.

249.
Write in the margins.

250.
Read between the lines.

251.
Enjoy the confusion.

252.
Cannibalize.

253.

Pledge allegiance off the map.

254.

Lose your critical distance—an uncolonized
position no longer exists.

255.

Design other worlds.

256.

Consider what reason excludes.

257.
Change the subject.

258.
Stop making sense.

259.
Flip flop.

260.
Fall into your politics through a series of
listless rejections.

261.

Leverage fictitious capital.

262.
Parody it all.

263.
Decorate your home as a sanctuary against the
speed of the world.

264.
Work without rules to find what rules your work.

265.
Fail to say what you mean.

266.
Produce only by reproducing.

267.
Put everything in quotes.

268.
Slack.

269.
Exploit banality.

270.
Tolerate the quaint naiveté of those who still
believe they can change the world.

271.
Forgo the desire for encyclopedic mastery.

272.
Read with an uncensored body.

273.
Question authorship.

274.
Obscure ownership.

275.
Move without changing your electronic address.

276.
Carve out one world.

277.

Use the word *post-modern*
without being quite sure whether
it is the dominant cultural logic
of late capitalism or pop-culture
shorthand for messy looking
buildings.

278.

Flip burgers.

279.

Draw your own maps.

280.

Don't write to say the last word.

281.

Watch out: philosophy is less truth than strategy.

282.
Manufacture intangibles.

283.
Discontinue.

284.
Speak with coded familiarity.

285.
Find beauty in the breakdown.

286.
Without essence or nation, compose an
ethnic identity.

287.
Stay mobile.

288.
Plagiarize yourself.

289.
Be a cyborg rather than a goddess.

290.
Present yourself as a flexible, highly skilled,
short-term commodity.

291.
Use puns to subvert the claims of seamless
meaning.

292.
Play with the pieces.

293.
Tune in to a televised town hall of tasteless intimacies.

294.
Resist closure.

295.
Author your desires.

296.
See what you believe.

297.
Beware of intellectuals who speak of Otherness
only amongst themselves.

298.

Negotiate truth.

299.
Blur genres.

300.
Disembody.

301.
Advance science by expanding the pool of
incompatible alternatives.

302.
Move the margins to the center.

303.
Break the frame.

304.
Bring back the aura.

305.
Amidst a permanent crisis in art, surrender
to the market.

306.
Review the reviewer.

307.
Buy time.

308.

Need speed.

309.

Remember: essence *is* only as essence *of*.

310.

Populate your wardrobe with corporate logos.

311.

Use one text to read another.

312.
Get along with each of your selves.

313.
Take casual labor seriously.

314.
Bullshit.

315.

Distrust photographic evidence.

316.

Lose the thread.

317.

Don't look for the center of power—
it's everywhere.

318.

Dabble in schizophrenia.

319.
Simulate.

320.
From the gaps, the margins, the boundaries—
resist.

321.
Recast the familiar until it demands explanation.

322.
Imagine contrary bodies.

323.
Travel abroad to find some suppressed aspect of
yourself on public display.

324.
Replicate.

325.
Know the sacred through pop.

326.
Have beliefs, but don't believe.

327.
Let anything go.

328.
Read classics and comics the same way.

329.
Suspect your commitments.

330.
Explore the richness of your limitations.

331.
Talk your own vernacular.

332.
Mutate.

333.
Zone for disparities in wealth.

334.
Play language games—your identity
depends on it.

335.
Code or be coded.

336.

Reschedule the crisis.

337.
©.

338.
Imitate old styles with new technology.

339.
Prepare to be misunderstood.

340.

In panicked defense of the sacred, embrace fundamentalism.

341.

Replace your career with multiple revenue streams.

342.

Log on to an electronic prosthesis.

343.

Make the border your territory.

344.
Impersonate yourself.

345.
Downsize.

346.
Upgrade.

347.
In an age of lost innocence, use irony to
speak of love.

348.

Derive that from which you once thought
all else derived.

349.

Traffic in novelty.

350.

Launch your critiques from a position of
inexcusable involvement.

351.

Listen closely: every story is a complex act of power.

352.
Be, like, whatever.

353.
Skip around.

354.
Hype.

355.
Dissect your intimate moments.

356.
Make the news.

357.
Reject general concepts.

358.
Multiply genders.

359.
Celebrate kitsch.

360.
Seek provisional truth.

361.
Stop waiting for Godot.

362.

Betray memory.

363.
Spawn new sensibilities.

364.
Continue to think and write even though reason is dead, history is over, the self is fractured, and knowledge is hopelessly enmeshed in oppressive relations of power.

365.
Practice one-liners.

⇒*Bibliography*⇐

True to the spirit of post-modernism, this is a work of inspired imitation. Credit is due to source texts, as follows:

Anderson, Walter Truett, ed. *The Truth About the Truth: De-confusing and Re-constructing the Postmodern World*. New York: Tarcher/Putnam, 1995.

Appignanesi, Richard, and Chris Garratt. *Introducing Postmodernism*. New York: Totem Books, 1995

Atkins, Robert. ArtSpeak: *A Guide to Contemporary Ideas, Movements, and Buzzwords*. New York: Abbeville Press, 1990.

Best, Steven, and Douglas Kellner. *Postmodern Theory: Critical Interrogations*. New York: Guilford Press, 1991.

Bukatman, Scott. *Blade Runner*. London: British Film Institute, 1997.

Computer Lab, The. *Beyond Cyberpunk!: A Do-It-Yourself Guide to the Future* (version 1.02). Louisa, VA: The Computer Lab, 1991.

Culler, Jonathan. *On Deconstruction: Theory and Criticism after Structuralism*. Ithaca: Cornell University Press, NY, 1982.

Bibliography

Dery, Mark. *Culture Jamming: Culture Jamming, Hacking, Slashing and Sniping in the Empire of Signs*. Westfield, NJ: Open Magazine Pamphlet Series, 1993.

Docherty, Thomas, ed. *Post-Modernism: A Reader*. New York: Columbia University Press, 1993.

Flax, Jane. *Thinking Fragments: Psychoanalysis, Feminism, and Postmodernism in the Contemporary West*. Berkeley, CA: University of California Press, 1990.

Frank, Thomas, and Matt Weiland, eds. *Commodify Your Dissent: Salvos from The Baffler*. New York: W. W. Norton, 1997.

Gergen, Kenneth. *The Saturated Self: Dilemmas of Identity in Contemporary Life*. New York: Basic Books, 1992.

Harvey, David. *The Condition of Post-Modernity*. Cambridge, MA: Blackwell Publishers, 1989.

Miller, Sarah. *Storytelling as Alchemy: Postmodernist and Feminist Approaches to History in the Fiction of Jeanette Winterson*. Unpublished undergraduate thesis, 1994.

Newman, Charles. *The Post-Modern Aura: The Act of Fiction in an Age of Inflation*. Evanston, IL: Northwestern University Press, 1985.

Ryan, Michael. *Marxism and Deconstruction: A Critical Articulation*. Baltimore, MD: Johns Hopkins University Press, 1982.

Sarup, Madan. *Introductory Guide to Post-Modernism and Post-Structuralism*. Athens: University of Georgia Press, 1993.

Bibliography

Sturrock, John. *Structuralism and Since*. Oxford, UK: Oxford University Press, 1979.

Taylor, Mark C., and Esa Saarinen. *Imagologies: Media Philosophy*. London: Routledge, 1994.

Wice, Nathaniel, and Steven Daly. *alt.culture: an a-to-z guide to the '90s—underground, online, and over-the-counter*. New York: HarperCollins, 1995.

Additional credit is due to the following authors and thinkers:
James Baldwin, Roland Barthes, Jean Baudrillard, Michael Berube, Jay Cantor, Gilles Deleuze and Felix Guattari, Jacques Derrida, Umberto Eco, Paul Feyerabend, Michel Foucault, Nancy Fraser and Linda Nicholson, Charles Jencks, Steiner Kvale, Donna Haraway, Ihab Hassan, bell hooks, Fredric Jameson, Jacques Lacan, Claude Levi Strauss, Robert Jay Lifton, Sabina Lovibond, Jean-Francois Lyotard, Martin Marty, Karl Marx and Friedrich Engels, Friedrich Nietzsche, Maureen O'Hara, Richard Rorty, Ferdinand de Saussure, Richard Shweder, William Simon, Robert Venturi, Paul Virillio, Cornel West.